One of the finest first books of recent years, Emily Sieu Liebowitz's *National Park* exhibits the emergent, wide-open verbal music of America's postmodern urban zones, those Yosemites and Yellowstones of second nature. Its collective, impersonal ways with voice and phrasing could be culled from the tattered margins of Ron Silliman's *In the American Tree*, that legendary anthology of Language Writing to which her title pointedly alludes. Liebowitz fabricates an enigmatic, quasi-personal mode in this arcade of poems evocatively composed for the page. A collection whose streets are littered with singular, verbally dense expressions and recursive poetic talismans, *National Park* moves the scales of our expectations in a poem. Liebowitz sends a "radio wave of creative space" like a quasar from some original precinct of the poetic universe.

DAVID LAU

I seldom want to read contemporary poems aloud, much less an entire book, but *this* book—I hear it in my mind's ear and want to say every word. *National Park* is a gorgeous discussion of the horrors of manifest destiny, plus ongoing everyday life (dancing, shopping) in the U.S. Step by carefully placed step, it brings us closer to gardens and buildings we feel like we've known forever but have already forgotten the names of. This is poetry for this century.

LUCY IVES

Emily Sieu Leibowitz's *National Park* is a kind of poetic field guide to fields. The map of the map *is* the map, mapping. "This is about logic, benchmarks, people gathered and circled." The ways we think in and of language become landscape, it's a national park after all. Liebowitz invites us to gather and circle, to meditate on the mediations, and find "the re-opened shacks in life."

ROD SMITH

Emily Sieu Liebowitz's *National Park* is the poetry of aspiration, and by aspiration, I mean breath, and by aspiration, I mean, to quote Nathaniel Mackey, "a wish, among others, to be we." Liebowitz beautifully attends to the line as a unit of breath, breaking it, extending it; each aerated line a horizon line that fades like a contrail. Liebowitz has written a haunting and mesmerizing series of eclogues to our vanishing west.

CATHY PARK HONG

National Park

National Park

Emily Sieu Liebowitz

NATIONAL PARK

BY EMILY SIEU LIEBOWITZ

COPYRIGHT © 2018

ALL RIGHTS RESERVED

PRINTED IN USA

ISBN 978-0-9987362-6-6

FIRST PRINTING

PUBLISHED BY GRAMMA

GRAMMA.PRESS

DISTRIBUTED BY SMALL PRESS DISTRIBUTION

SPDBOOKS.ORG

COVER IMAGE: 'INTAGLIO,' FROM PORTFOLIO ONE © 2005 CLAIRE COWIE

Section I

DAYS THAT BREAK   5

TOWARD DECORATION   8

OUTSIDE SUCKS   9

AN ODE: YOU NEVER FORGET HOW TO RIDE A BIKE   11

AFTER *HOARDERS* ON A&E   14

CHIEF CONCERNS   15

A DOWNTOWN RECOLLECT   17

FRAMED/MAIMED ABOUT   18

BEFORE THE COLOR RUNS OUT   19

REOCCURRING OBJECT   21

YOUR FACE LIKE MOON FACE   24

Section II

AS I SIT IN A RENTED HOUSE 27

NOBODY HAS TO KNOW 28

GOOD CIRCUMSTANCE 30

FOUND ON THE STREET 32

OF THIS ACT 34

I GO ONTO MOMENT 36

AN ACTUAL MONUMENT 38

A WAIT TO BE FOUND 39

HALCYON DAYS 40

BREATH AND ITS FOUR WALLS 41

LOCATER OF MOVEMENT 43

HAPPY TO BE YOURS 44

HOMESICK POEM 45

WAKE ME UP FOR FRIDAY 46

Section III

FOR THE RICH KIDS 49

MOON CONSPIRACY 51

GONE TO HIDE / HOW TO PARTY 52

THE AFFAIRS OF MEN 55

TODAY THEY TRIED TO BLOW UP THE MOON 56

THIS HAS NOTHING TO DO 57

LATE IN THE GAME 59

LUNCH WITH FRIENDS 60

FRAME WRONG / PICTURE CENTURIES 64

TRAINED STEMS 67

I AM ALWAYS LEAVING TO GATHER THE NEWS 69

Acknowledgments
Author

Wait!

Wait a minute Mr. Postman

Wait!

Wait Mr. Postman

Please Mr. Postman, look and see

If there's a letter in your bag for me

Please Mr. Postman

You know it's been so long

THE MARVELETTES

Days That Break

News that keep sails taut on the we

                    we are

conversation, big rough battle we are

roots to roofs: this could be poison,

          this plant suffocation, the frame we were

               the strictures our charm.

Extinction we are, exterior bridge sight I am

               earthquake constructing commuters, together

             it was, lonely west we were, middle

sending space to subdue.

Dew catching sleep we were

        liking things, doing things they are

important. I felt

          like sitting here, I am

facing these lovers of order, obeying topography in my

crawling canvas circus strewn sky.

Fruit stands we were

      Cupressus macrocarpa we are

                      concerned

with the glistened private they are

a disengaged prison, halfway hotels, hilltop grocers

         singled we were

westward eroding.

Splintered into small business

                  we are

I fissures, the large forest we were,

      the factories we were

the broken trip I was making frames

               over main street.

It is too early to be so wise,

      look again at the weather we are

the landlessness we were

      the news outside the hallways outside it goes

where we were.

Early time catastrophe I am

alternately held and released,

pre-fire we once were city centralized. I am

committed to Pacific fades we are

home ethnographed into proverbs:

hatchmen passing the American lexicon,

docking your boats we were

splendor peddling blame from cold colonies I am

tight lipped scaffolds.

Postcard:

I am

in crumble we were

on the edge as we are

bringing fault lines I am, fogged into the new noise.

Long way commons we have

gone cold I have.

Alarm clock set we were: 7 A.M.

Toward Decoration

The previous pace lacked any road that did not circle a monument.

But a monument circles like addiction:

carries backless beating that tugged with the taste of reigned surface—a home in which it belongs.

It is confounded in grandeur, quieter than a squeak composed when the finger pressed thrown pieces of an ancient accident asking an age for opportunity:

larger than mountain means to call, left endless in a crumble place.

On top it flies because of gold, about speed it cracked causing kicks in the space above. The startled sea circled like distraction.

Outside Sucks
I THINK I'M GONNA TAKE A NAP...

We're blown away when young begins, addicts

trained to tinker toys.

Look up!

there is something imaginary like thought, like the governor.

The subway is coming, it bellows, "flightless gazaland, caves at this angle have it,

perfect."

Excess stripping telephone wire intestine:

the password is Darfur.

With water we used to go to museums, now abducted

children news power, currents penciled in the walk around.

One wall, meaningful, but they check your bag.

Rehearsing lettered confrontation: we spoke, faces against stone,

masonry fractured with requests, simple spun wool and what it beckons:

sandy climbs   served to order and soundless.

Sunday is a homeless landscape. Empty electrons and their security blankets.

This is about logic, benchmarks, people gathered and circled.

Hand on my shoulder, how one enters,

inches away the table (now we are in a place {oak molding and a mahogany foyer} stirs a

present pipe of recall

('pipette' drops sensations, a bridge, woo woo for public transportation).

Stand amongst collected pennies, a sad coin

of carcass, of a sentimental highway

in the desert, winds scrapping weeds

away...

As my friend explains: pretense is ears and a globe sounds

"you are old man with your guitar, you are old, actual and dim."

An Ode: You Never Forget How to Ride a Bike

Mailman, forget your letters outside is doing fine,

       crooning snow color they say

you look fine, anyway.

Crooning archway encouraged acoustic. People here for swindle, their leather-faced

leaflets left behind. Bells—it's lunchtime. Open metal measure, time piece

yacht me home flawless. The foghorn. The brought back.

                Paved face, masons come back now. It is our erratic wall,

                   forgetting its post.

I trade here for another day.

                        A relief—

                        city filled garage sale, misshaping memory as metropolis
sidewalks sparkle recycled, safekeeping, special boxes
stacking stalked
buoying up the slipping bells. Twilights force entry. The frontier that is done, lazy, and
fancy.

Outside is okay. Different salt, sidewalked still leaving bay salt topologizing.
I have this advantage.
It's a free ride and they are leading a
disco across. Take naps, bring blankets.

Winter weather kit, the lost quaintness of locales bitten against brick, against the hauntless side panels. Mountains, where are the pragmatic protections? I am wind-worn.

Whittled down mechanics,
light up this range, relive the bells told time.
Come out of your canyons, come off your ship.
The seagoing grainy, marbling marshlands fragile replacement, the channels out chiming edible fields—

Some swell, some antenna's field
whittled edible
field.
The packed clouds are maximized
The estate tax I attend, I forget.

After *Hoarders* on A&E

Telephone wires talk apart. Operator museumed. Decisions are everywhere, boxing allusion. All my trouble stems from this: melted hindsight arcs, history and its bins. Homeland, we are safe to feel again, to construct enough, opposite enough, to perceive that flat ranged line. I am in this. You are in my pocket, you are in my room. Come back for a while. I'll keep you in my pocket, I'll keep you in my room. I have been waiting as hindsight hallways allusion. I have always been like this. Please don't leave me alone. I wasn't always like this. Emergence racing, roles imposing, documents edging to feel again behind familial containment. Inevitable generated insensitive logic. What kind of child is this?

Chief Concerns

Seen past in every

turn, looking at the music stretching

stopped.

A portioned sleep rings

relations. Happening

        here hospiced place.

Standard schizophrenic

streets extending lines to

hidden controls expanse

beat out gliding

notes on the wind milled

ground.

Any chances left

        on calm spots,

struggle pushes against, a hand stopped in

its owned motion, but spatters leave

pavement shrouded.

Spiked bullets amount

in numbers, not bodies

layering the promise of

timetables.   Nixon is a liar.

The piles encounter life circling

          itself, loosing

     edges to round

the world. The tour manipulates

     length.   Flying with chance

of refolding.   Laws here, unfortunately

washing, half there.

A Downtown Recollect

Version freshens what we see
        building blends conjecture, conceding
a familiar trace.

How this works is a different latch
      pulling unstable ruins to make decay—

        evolution, the best of what is made methods into antique
prisoned to a pressurized particular.

Hauntless crawls
        easeled scrawl of far:
this old leaf, dark in its hidden yellows,
        dumpster dives for flowers tendering tasted—
        the perfect house
to blow arrival homeless.

Framed/Maimed About

Road contraction confession: I am a cardboard captain whaling overfished land to bring hunted horizons of sun. Either side passing nooses for a collective dangle. I got only time. My walk stops when my muscles crumble. A donated tree as a cultural gift corrals difference to blossom, seasons other into interned. Consistent diorama. Never left neighborhood can go places: stuff photographs into a double pane: stoop roof's radius of who I am alone. A base line. An arc. Fog driven antenna—artifacts are for tourists, allowing older, eliciting scene.

Before the Color Runs Out

Motions grow larger, weave into wading around empire, a wait to

San Francisco meant to point as most

when looked across water.

It named itself gates branching expand.

I strike here.   Slipping off my shoes

heirlooms of flowers wonder reigning halo over my head.

He was red and said he was gold, year
elaborating false color.

A lined knife scrapes forehead and rips off the scalp—this is particular, kempt hair to tie on
a
belt.

Blankets do not carry heat but

distance, and terms not present

but time.

An edge on a globe is safety of
an end screams, "the whole world is watching."

Changes opposite breath, here, similitude.

We carry
home on fringes,   hearts   hearts of   heartless   flowers

                                        margined from blank, Eastern Europe, New
York.
                              Fissures as arms exceed my joints. The peace was a
              full choice   causing forward depression.
A man
is about
to be shot in a photograph.

Reoccurring Object

Radio wave of created space

working cobweb over every day steps.

I need base stair

         traversing

         where I need to go.

         I tell this place:

I need guns   I need grain.

But when I wake

         my mailman never brings them to me.

                  USPS is a time tease

             to scream my dreams of bartering

Welled in polis, elongated ice plant trail

                                                benefits,

            like uprooting trees

                    planting them to the left and watching them grow.

                    Mailman back
            like he could bring news.

            Now in my hand there are coupons
                            where nothing used to be.

I heard they are taking Saturday away.

It makes no difference.

Me and my stamp collection:
tribe of built

people arranging into
fireplace décor.

Friends—please be here with me.

to find ourselves later...

going to look up...

Your Face Like Moon Face

Wrangling the bend, the coat of arms caught a
splayed sphere, swinging crackled. Just the leftover
atrium of the otherwise prairie.

And it comes to its audience
and keeps company with friends.
The train yard, the territories—I am with you,

you have entered my dreams and sat with me at suppertime.
Try to explain to this crowd, barter reason,
point out that the new mood is all torn up.

It churns ruins' river potable. It becomes
public square foresight, a big-band edict.
Just cement maneuvers contracting weaves

of wrinkled boughs, bending closer
all these friends that are so far off shore.
This mood mentioned apologies. Corn fields.

Followed forts pathway attack I should give
Nebraska a better chance. They are so sorry.
I am sorry too. We are all just sun-chasing fools.

SECTION II

As I Sit in a Rented House

Distance happens

      pastures of nations coming and going

into inland ports attention, ancient seas, where I lay my head, etc.

Timed in pathways, Lincoln Highway marker, scenic byways

      journeying scaffolds over small town's skillfully measured

          seasonal charm.

Mild temperatures linking me westward, marine layers meditating middle,

   calmed levels of erosion erasing traces previous

         I could not have been here first.

If it is claimed, parsed, reconfigured,

      etc., could new men do new things, use limits, industrialize figures,

         organize principals, help me frame where I am actually going?

      I am not at war with this exhibition:

         sense revering flattened vantages. I am

creeping around wiring intertwining margins to dominate views

ribboning sight: harpooned cargo ships sight

evergreen docked to my still place, watch tides

         drift in real times.

Torrents

      torturing me from this sweep away, I sit so far away.

Nobody Has to Know

Collection of who,

       thing I am,

melts concessions of recollect,

       helicopters progress,

calls out memorized.

I'll be different this time
be present—I will
      alongside perennials
           spin in stalls
        of walled in
          temporary

      ending sometimes

      in stairwell construction.

This scalp collection,
       it anchors to announced places—

model towns and their
      strategic purposes.

      A trailway synapse
a second of cenotaph
elevating
every time I should
have asked you to dance.

Good Circumstance

Citizens' turmoil, stay

for   the   shifting

ground crawls to balance.

       I reached myself wayward.

Street names localize. I

                still can't speak Spanish or

       squash waves peaking

          currents, machined tapered

slits arriving on sunned winter,

       the day to be born.

          Engines of stroked highlights

       propped   and   structured in

refraction.   Frame for shatter

       windows on screened, infinite

possibilities in finite gears:

fathers are country   reject

       both for antique clouds

passing.   Backwards the

       heavily honored

          time,   horizon twists

towards places,

weather,

we gather in the fissures.

Found on the Street

Caught on natural heights,
I point to the left
say, "That side of the freeway
is where we buy drugs."

Shreds of relative
hidden in a rural house.
Screening
basement's hold of boxed means,
scraps of where you were on my furniture;
tenseless.

It was nice to feel

        prisoned in expected ways, to

   watch a slow speech

     sloth dead into dying.

Watch a different you

bomb them and put them in camps.

A statue out front operates remnant:

caging icons drilled rhythms

      redrawing one room to

     see it not work

        hammering a simple hum:

Pick it up. Call

a friend. Tell them

you love them.

Of This Act

People and their big music,
people like their big government.

                Washed gates breaking down
        summer sport waiting:
margins glass historians,
            New Yorker cartoons
of witty citizens show me

        naturalization is a specified child.

Trembling intensive irrigations

reinforce   tributaries.

        Everywhere is expensive—
policing defamiliarized

flashback newsflash
        cities bounce back from ignored arid.

Billboards supplement ports attention for downtown.
        Liquefaction loosens the looms:
exposition city, comeback kid

strangling infant dust.

The confused clock sundials international
                shadows, sewing domestic fissures.

And arrival
foretells safety in numbers—

taming shaken houses into crashing walls.

I Go onto Moment

I've done nothing this month, decades
continue and there are still places that
perpetuate.
Villages wave flags dismantled and
on the street generational
lamentations make a continental courtyard.

I am roped in. I go on sense-giving tours,
walked around by guides strangling their
lungs
                singing anything
                to make something sung.
                Following them all over town, an echo
of a forgotten song, "in my dreams I've been in love."

Too long I have been awake, and, with you, come upon land,
            cutting ourselves off and
cutting our own throats—sutures sliding
the streamlined wind
our skyscrapers narrow.

En route, I am travelling to the hymn that
was once found.
The mountainous ballads, springing around
the people we were and the beloved we
grieve.
Alongside, the public comes riding into

town, around trapped ears
to answer, the honor is in how we hold, honing
instance to   our balcony seats.

An Actual Monument

Sunday opens itself, scurrying though it remains.

Tired of lint breaking, the day closes calling itself a kind of grain

a burrow amongst taxicabs and telephone wires.

I stake in a positioned pour, a window lung

enters pointed towards left because I am the passed call,

counting slight rapids charging my hands.

Daring to teach of swim, a center, I began

redwoods sprouting at the roots. Mono Lake or winter, both waterless

today, but in yesterday they were alive, a lied absent.

A captured here strains cotton into cypress,

begins home along longer hours.

I shorten again. Frontier or night—they shrink into pressured strangle.

The current undersides every road and spills onto the sidewalk.

Dusk shoots into a swirl of ice cubes begging to lament.

A Wait to Be Found

Let slide ladders ring on steep staircases.
A curled formula: there, always. I sit
bayless for the first time, a river to
lake they all imply ocean.

I curate bodied land, tying grey steps
when they stood self-reflexive—a glitter
listing to control the tide. Glued together
beat envelopes a contorted wishless list.

Stomped current, I expand waves' breaking—fractures
furthering long waste inside landings. Drawn
lines barring direction to ebb, expanding
together the slanted straining of horizon.

Flat mist-stained texture bridges every
trapped hue under troubles: iron hours
spring foam. Pleased in flowering circles
a cursed rapid, turns growth into foreign bricks.

Crashed on sharp rungs, frontiers slid buoys to
distance. Slips are a box of implied silver.
Promises a hint of height: an edge. It said,
"gather on that edge".

Breath and Its Four Walls

Origin has

> long-term effects.

On a country road I walk
and it concaves construction.

> On the pier, a man pushes air into bottles
and sells a traced drift of silent.

> Tonics for cold unsorted sleep,
he captures and barters

> bridged presence, and one can
carry away a small
piece of science shaking,

a caramel-colored bottle containing the frequent failure of fact.

I have its picture in my arms:

> a framed continent of finite,
the spent confetti of a carnival,
wandering partitions on a

careless crawl,
gating
a version of same: a face, a form.

Halcyon Days

The difference in two
lines pebbles into certain
scaffolds. Direct to topple
numbing: a call to letters—stare out—called to a toy expanse.

It tinkers, as young as
it is, switching names to
A — reached shadow to find
its runaway. A wait to watch grid locked scaffolds go to war.

Blue the white rising to
double onto it-
self. Fade as gradation

A comforts to stay in low lands.

I never imagined hidden as new,
to relay know
on a point unwinds Skyscrapers to do not, do exist.

Lead tends to open
possibilities: elements a
pyramid, all strive metallic texture,
centered, gold sheen a point, but its place consists in pressure.

No one coming to replace glass any day. I package. It lied, there was never anyone.

Houses may shape in satin, dress in crisping.
Watched valley lines up a slow curve, dusk
into grains, 5 minutes. The sun carries before on.

Locater of Movement

Pronounce step now shaking, wears up for down,
near buttons bubble to surface, skimming
feigned seascape, bars on windows sleeve not to
sound. You chase, the boat circles.

Jump in front, heavy jacket, hold light
in your hands. Who doesn't see the rocks glow?
Alone for miles, this warning sight stalking hours.

The shrines posted on top warned against shallow water.
Towers hide behind coasted symptoms, rising to sand
glistening to shadow,
shadow washing moss.

Happy to Be Yours

Strained, heavy, back
it forces its weaves into
any window. This is one
side of a hill. East appeared—

appeared an original, never courted
as horizon. I-specific bridge,
consider its across, a shake to only
people in distance.

Every sound is a foghorn. From
far away everything looks like
one person, drowned in fortune

I bury in this side of mountain crumble,
plating this place to a demonstration: of timed gaps crashing.

Homesick Poem

This middle country center is sad land,
lending hauntless flat land that
wagoned death, picking up sticks to tie
forts together with twine winter.

Painted future is a Pacific fade
possibilities echoing parsed
colors to hang on before it
comes circling round again. Horizon

halts what seen can bring,
strings of highway numbering what it is
to know, to sprout already. Branching
landscape, bridges gate chaparrals' collapse,

spun goldspun in its weighted resting, loosens
the across. Bay-iron levels of
manmade mention Oakland.
At underneath there is there,

everywhere matters, all sides of a
hill are a mountain—a steep braided into
expanse, a city sewn to see the
sun surrendering west away.

Wake Me Up for Friday

Come museum, show your captors,
teach us to greet the sometimes other.

I am learning. I am being educated
to carry chasms as you arrange them in my arms.

Mid-trip, eruption mounts exhibition,
a pavilion plays the jungle-gardens that
speak so pretty,

sounding out stone moments,
that fall to the court useless and
unseen. Information moves

the remainder, an echolocation. Imprisoned,
jailed geography

leaves us to where travel went.
And how it used to be, without me,
an already furnished crowded elsewhere.

For The Rich Kids

Thrown candy on the ground, fake old
school penny candy, general
that misused place of sundries should
be bartering blankets into
grain, wheat into mules instead is
a hand full of candy buttons.

Jungle condemned toss. Thrown soldiers
lobbing nation candy into
crowds of children begging, misled
catches corroding bodied by
misshappening memorials.
Fancy wrapped tide shifts, conditional

confectioned dulled out informative
results count, dioxin dealt out
by standing flight patterns sending
thrown pieces of people. A scavenge
later into the leaves of the
airplane dropped parade, checking to look

for any candy left behind.
Permissionless life styles, adult
gets whatever one wants: like
metermaidless street riding can
wake us ticketless, obscuring
all of the known ingredients

to candy.

Moon Conspiracy

Where I strayed, I stayed in a lied lunar
landing. The tides tormented twitching
eddy twirls, ridden evenings to sleep time.
Water possibilities make me tired, watching
weather though an interned aquifer.

What I watched I scraped through, weakening
structures meant to mimic
letter writing time. It is effort
to rake up autumn, gathering piles, pyres of where
I've been in temporal turmoil. A blaze to collect

tideless evolutions, walking upright
against flags waving still. I was in a place: photographed
bedside a different gallery: pictured westward,
projected tide, beginning and begun
eroding further what is already away.

      Trailed out wrinkling
electric yard signs.
      look around!   there are tangible things!
motel figures
      shared technologies

left over water fallen sky.

Gone to   Hide
How to   Party

Daily sorts

support   limbless

disagreements   scene: local

house haunted

       lenses soldiering space

           erect mourning

Keep going

           frame correction

Keep going

           transcontinental lame

Enough mountains pound

       sprinkles into tiny towns:

       murder petals end

       punishing stalls to beach looms

       formed season other

Inherited horizon mutilates mask

trumpets   tapping   to

carry difference

they tap

          occupied present

over and over

sliding this spun past

Corralled cycles leak sharp

points   carry artifact:

limit signal present pulse: empty

boxes

          heaving heavies

of hurried color

hanging

Elect of

relative killed   bones swinging

porch and rafters

          farm image bleeding contempt

          to prize must mean memory

returns more than its got

Go on

          covered seams

Grow on

          lonely crime:

break apart singled: shorter

flag safety could be

        slits to a

parapet—there is nowhere

else to go   pipes geography

like   a   five year old

Bringing

          fold

Bring it

          ancient

Legend conversation

a post   to come

back   to circling

structures   surround

paint-gardens   branching cornered

into broken

Make up mind

        with thatch roof envy

wakes with heads hanging

bodies

          missing

complications

inviting taped sections to parade

The Affairs of Men

way back, sight forms

     what is forced to be seen.

A corner to clutter,

falling upon

                "a shape in what must be

       when we close our eyes,   a balancing act of naptime colors:

        spun temporarily of screamed edges, rounding

      falls into waking with too many direct perspectives to follow.

Here I am in this,

     me in love with every room,

          drunk on all we have.

From my city to yours—

    Old Man, you taught, the world has arrived, and

    I am giving you a present

    you and your tansy both.

Today They Tried to Blow Up the Moon
...HOW EMBARRASSING

Squirrel on my roof, mouse in my wall

suspending architecture's crumbling chaos.

Charmless lean years of interest scraping

shadowless walls, I am engrossed in

somebody else's haunt. Interrupted made place somebody makes

caught. There are countless blinks

wandering around a to-do list of told things.

I house westward things, scavenge erupting groundwork

lapping that which was brought. I sold my furniture.

The scrape across squirrels across the continued shear stress,

crackling a culturally conduced communal end. Interstate lifestyle

limits views scrape to a telephone wire trapeze act:

some forced hallucination commanding qualities that rely on

greenhouse grown personality traits. They bay at me,

be quiet today, do not know these people.

This Has Nothing to Do

We, city to make

    beautiful days, turn

    struggle into murals.

    Ruins of spiked red

brushes strain to

say, "pleasure takes

hung space: ambiguous

hint of breakdown.

      the first representation

swallowing sound.

Some call today, some step down

is occurring. No shift. A basement,

we may miss relation.

    Broke frames of graded,

      we begin as

    both, bare with

    hammer in hand. A has

barriers to rebuild: sad, lost.

Blood to other, it is

it is not, this is too global:

You. Enemy. There.

I. Me. Here

changing   scaffolds

it is already happening

Late in the Game

Stationed to search houses,

they found nothing

but the charm of an abandoned house.

Clever window work, I step on

everyday. Weakening locked habit.

Irrigated and addicted. Expanse

has to be more than movie's westward dance hall.

I won't stay here

landlocked in anxiety. Let me

burrow into peaking perspective.

I will do anything. I will order

a drink and let the boys be everything.

Lunch with Friends

Cranes lifting cargo to contain carried difference unpacking foreign to bury the same.

      Mint is a tower, an old roof, quaked and erupting without warning:

we will rebuild

we will bring gray

translate this field sequence into eastern standard.

      To ride over the world freshens fear as locatable, dropped edges

           give us

      gated water, old ferry water, sediment water

to frame shattered

happenings

      bridged in collapse:

    lattice of worn

      runaway margins.

We will

bare threat,

        beaching nation to an end, to a

shifted ground grinding landscape and its language into lies.

Bound circles

        hold sight

as it pours a familiar portrait of a shrieking frontier.

Mountain pans currency for gold, mishears mined lumber lasting leagues, membered

land we can't abandon when fortune looks hitchhiked from yellow grass growing origin.

The past is too tight.

We gaze scaffolded,

skyscraper sells obligation to represent shaken already, carries into distance a new
native of wreath

       one can see distorting
self-centered
       colonial same time
           came to link.

A wandering migratory wafted in westward direction of funeral perspective.

Mummified media birth is the axis mourning: a haunting of telegraph tribesman,
primitive isolate of technology twisting towards.

Photo reproduces future as hallucination, controls tide to torrent, blazes ambivalent into
grout growing proximity.

It's too late.

Transplants extend

        supply ships small settlements

           psychotic proportions

              send out

      sketches inspiring scene

                    ocean surrounds visible as harbor shelters
temporary fort attacking natural ports opposing national monument wagoning hoarded
quiet elongating hours landed in a constant crumble of commemorate.

We will scape views as coastal fog causes grain to rust.

We will have newspapers operate nostalgia, do drugs and make suicide pacts, make love
and hope we don't get cancer.

Frame Wrong
Picture Centuries

Maybe we should not hear it: I am not ready

to let go of this continental shelf, gripping hold to any edge.

I want to be roadway-ready, how post-office-ready rewards this heavy

space smothering us. Already spoked margins

milling carved out windows for this perfect view.

The way it grows is shot wartime

turning primetime gears: empty

street execution: flinch ready, cover-ready

social haunt-ready.   We always have it wrong

ready to place it on our coffee table interests.

Address: we are massacre-ready: shackled breath, breathing back

momentless triggers: they should build monuments already:

twisting direction into frozen already.

Like great war days that pass synthesizing

this army base backyard. Present received,

floundering we process, bayoneted with arms

ready to waste any body into duress.

Shoot,   we are ready to perch on any porch

slaying small worlds into heads hanging:

old ways hanging bodyless haunt:

accumulating already, decomposing already
this imaged protest as it produces a
man kindling himself into fire: stuck in motion-ready
reeled-into-already: palpable horizoned ready:

promoting ash soaken limits into large scales:
continuous tones screened tormenting.
Scheduled old-way-ready, I have no room
for this half captured point of error. I am on such a shore

       wintering already,

and I have stood up for you already, paid attention, poured grout
into places permanent change has yet to come,
shaking you ready to meet me at my door.

Trained Stems

Lawns clogged, river rise up beyond ravines: design drowns valley's owned, rounded growth: concrete pipes soothed after getting directions:

gently scaffold: we build gray, we
build to move:
not brick-bound basements settled in
deep centers: a jump across planes:
seen expanse
is pointed nation
is pointed nation as numbers: cause arms chewing to own
condition: snow   stalling as   an ill- fated shoes his month siding mountain
crumble.

    one can see the city: boat to wagon, spokes loosen the place: arrival stories edible
    deaths as the west's:
                    tires hugging chains to touch the enriched
          ground:

Canals cut length, tie strengthening in request, pulsate,

carry happenings

between bombs offered. Termites tasting forts intended action standing

against opposite oceans' mediation on

fluid weapons attacking, the end of eating.

Eyes mural youthful monuments—

not   right

this   second.   A following, floundered a current wayward division, roomed and

blended process of pre-fixed porting.

Abandon the base coastline: the empty holes were calibrated for a mechanized enemy—

deserted bunkers impressing threat to beach: curving blue lines hanging sight to hold

there.

Refracted ebbing reoccurred on constructed throats.

Collective, we need

events, familiar as news, helicopters, spotlight,

the reopened shacks in life

form. We buy vials of dirt. Two gold flakes in. Pour our sit with buggies. Pan for gold.

I Am Always Leaving to Gather the News

I sit there, I go away, I let pavement push

against. Epicenter converses shifting. 1906 loops

translation from universally understood spatial

signifiers, tremors card games from a competitive

streak. Documentation spokes plaintive

thoughts through aggregate arrivals. A wafted neighborhood

arranged into a fleeting horizon. Bills are resource,

design axioms our limbs clean. I hand

wash my clothes because machines clamor:

down coat, wool scarf, conventional glove wearing

weather. I am tired of this. I take public transportation.

The tacked down rush-off of the crowd detonates—

It screams, "goodbye radio, goodbye wave/particle confusion,"

We are ready—paradigm,

I have provided California, and I am losing my balance,

lesser phenomena drowning my eyes to a tear.

Expansion of dryland farming is an effigy of my year.

Taken space enlarges nothing, a tacked down

itemized account of Fort Kearny's informational center.

Camping on each landing comes with its own national

anthem, a staircase humming, "goodbye continents,

goodbye immaculate overthrow." We've been carried

along in motion, herded into direction, given

brochures along the way. I deserve better than this: a window

unwinding, fending off a constant apology, born too late

to mobilize, dismantling basic feature.

Highway infrastructure traverses dead weight,

the Portola Expedition, mailbox grouping. Things we have

in common converses boring like, "goodbye protoplasmic

centuries, goodbye radiating land run incentives."

This sentimental farewell is a centrifuge finishing school,

a miniature 2010 census envelope.

A moment magnitude parades my home full of houseplants.

I don't do anything.

They just grow.

THANK YOU TO THE EDITORS OF THE FOLLOWING JOURNALS IN
WHICH SOME OF THESE POEMS HAVE APPEARED: *FOG MACHINE,
THE IOWA REVIEW, LANA TURNER, LIFE & DEATH IN AMERICAN
CITIES, LVNG, RESEVOIR, SHAMPOO MAGAZINE,* AND *THE WEST
WIND REVIEW.* I AM ESPECIALLY GRATEFUL TO THE SONG CAVE
FOR PUBLISHING THE CHAPBOOK, IN ANY MAP, COMPRISED OF
POEMS FROM THIS BOOK.

THANK YOU, GRAMMA.

THANKS TO THE IOWA WRITERS' WORKSHOP AND THE ALBERTA
METCALF KELLY FELLOWSHIP FOR THE TIME & SPACE.

TO THESE PEOPLE THIS BOOK IS INDEBTED & I AM GRATEFUL:
TOBY BROTHERS, OSSIAN FOLEY, SAMUEL GROSSMAN, MARK
LEVINE, BENJAMIN LIEBOWITZ, NATHANIEL MACKEY, AMANDA
NADELBERG, GEOFFREY G. O'BRIEN, ROD SMITH, COLE SWENSEN,
NICK TWEMLOW, & EMILY WILSON. SPECIAL THANKS TO DAVID LAU,
WITHOUT WHOM I COULD NOT HAVE WRITTEN THESE POEMS.

EMILY SIEU LIEBOWITZ GREW UP IN THE SAN FRANCISCO BAY AREA.
A GRADUATE OF THE IOWA WRITERS' WORKSHOP, SHE CO-EDITS
LVNG MAGAZINE AND LIVES IN BROOKLYN, NY.

#1 *Ugly Time*, by Sarah Galvin

#2 *Community Garden for Lonely Girls*, by Christine Shan Shan Hou

#3 *(v.)*, by Anastacia-Reneé

#4 *Safe Word*, by Donald Dunbar

#5 *Reflexiones junto a tu piel*, by Diana Morán (trans. Ash Ponders)

#6 *Soap for the Dogs*, by Stacey Tran

#7 *A Machine Wrote This Song*, by Jennifer Hayashida

#8 *National Park*, by Emily Sieu Liebowitz